A Few Interiors

ROWLAND BAGNALL was born in Oxfordshire in 1992. He studied English at St John's College, Oxford, and completed an MPhil in American Literature at the University of Cambridge. His poetry and reviews have appeared in various publications, including *Poetry London*, the *Los Angeles Review of Books* and *New Poetries VII* (Carcanet). He lives and works in Oxford.

ROWLAND BAGNALL

A Few Interiors

CARCANET

First published in Great Britain in 2019 by
Carcanet Press Ltd
Alliance House, 30 Cross Street
Manchester M2 7AQ
www.carcanet.co.uk

A CIP catalogue record for this book is available from the British Library.
ISBN 978 1 784107 35 2

The publisher acknowledges financial assistance from Arts Council England.

Supported by
ARTS COUNCIL
ENGLAND

Typeset in England by XL Publishing Services, Exmouth
Printed and bound in England by SRP Ltd, Exeter

Contents

I

II

for my parents

I

But as I travelled hither through the land,
I find the people strangely fantasied,
Possessed with rumours, full of idle dreams,
Not knowing what they fear, but full of fear.
                    Shakespeare, *King John*, 4.2.143–146

Glider

after Peter Lanyon

Without knowing how or why
      like trying to remember exactly where
you were exactly this time a year ago
      the launch cable detaches
from the substance of the ground below
      below the white and blue of the sea or sky
a distanceless shape opening and closing
      with a kind of rushed completeness
and if this had been a failure
      what exactly did I mean by that?

Like breathing into a mouth that doesn't
      breathe back or slamming on the brakes
on icy roads covered in salt and grit
      could you sense a delay
between the two and even if you
      manage to distinguish them
what do you get?

      Making each time the same pattern
or the same pattern reversed
      everything was as we thought it would be
except that nobody looked like they wanted
      to be where they were
as if they'd simply wandered
      into (or almost out of) the picture
by mistake, that line almost bending
      over itself before it thins
and rises up again into a sword
      if *sword*'s the word.

We stood there for ages,
watching it all accumulate, the little
   shudders lingering like new clouds
over wooded hills. As for everything else,
      winding and unwinding hugely,
filling out the sky, there was a sense
   we'd seen it all before, only
      in passing or in blinding light.

Viewpoint

In *Rear Window* (1954), Alfred Hitchcock suddenly looks at us
through the glass frame of an apartment penthouse, somehow
somewhere other than behind the camera's lens – viewed from
the perspective of James Stewart's binoculars – all but invisible
to anyone who doesn't know it's him. *Always make the audience
suffer as much as possible,* I thought, rains beginning on the roof.

From up here I could see a skydiver looking backwards at a plane
as if it was falling away from him and not the other way around.
The air was the same temperature as I was, still breathable and
warm but lightly thickening with something else, like vapours
pouring slowly from a car's exhaust. Away to the right I swore
I could see the monstrously reclining figures of a sculpture park,

misshapen and decayed, the stones displaying marks left by
the hurricanes of several years ago. Around the moment of
deployment, the parachutist feels a brief instance of shock
between the pulling of the ripcord and successful opening
of the main canopy. Convinced the mechanism has finally
failed, he tries to recall a succession of emergency techniques

before – at last – the canvas swells, jerking freefall to violent
and relieving halt. Throughout the film, a pianist composes
a song called 'Lisa'. His voice is never heard; we witness him
in long shots through the window. He seems to live alone but
for the one-time appearance of the filmmaker standing several
feet behind him, winding an old clock on the mantelpiece.

Evening in Colorado

Something unwinds and breaks, spilling glass across the room.
It takes time to establish that a thing's not there – noise, stars,
excitement, grief – like the shutting-off of certain lights.

I remembered having been to Florida as a child,
but could only really summon up the glare of heat on roads,
a beach, and a skyline of durationless hotels.

We had a rental car with cruise control, which I remember
thinking drove itself. But now from up here I see everything,
the city like a signal on the verge of fading out.

I drank a bottle of 'tropical' flavoured liquid and sat down
on the bed, thinking about my brothers – thousands
of miles away in several directions – staring through

the window at a bright display of grand pianos,
an old cinema, and the empty space a building used to be.
A group of children ran around through jets of water.

Something unwinds and breaks: like a morning? silence?
cables? arms? During the night I woke up to an accident
and lay there motionless beneath the ceiling fan.

Total Recall

We have gone for
weeks without sound.

We have ordered
and eaten
bowlfuls of
pistachio ice cream.

We have dyed
our hair
magnificent shades
of red and gold,
strolling
the suburban
streets and gardens
which are full
of life.

We have borrowed
and lost your longest
HDMI cable.

We have surrendered
untold barbecues
still sticky with
congealing fat.

We have drawn a
detailed map
of the surrounding
area, or how
we wish
that area to
look.

We have lit
the major
public parks,
now
awash with
coloured lights.

We have
flensed
and cooked
a stranding
whale, taking its
skeleton, bone
by giant, hulking
bone, and hurling
it into the sea.

We have watched
the days
fall equally
away, the nights
hot with the taste
of ash.

We have sent out
countless messages
and wait to
see what they
return.

We have gone for
weeks without sound.

We have been thinking
to ourselves about
the final thing we
may've heard.

Hothouse

In the right context, *forever* can mean
anything. Completely out of context, it means *space*.
In my new notebook I write *drown*, then
on a new line *balcony*.

I picture my veins bursting like an over
-pressured dam, pouring away, Old Testament red.
In my new notebook I write *Old Testament red*, then
on a new line *double doors*.

I want my notes to be a poem about the different
kinds of pain: loss of love, loss of loved one, etc.

In the right context, forever *can mean / anything,*
it starts, the summer folding over itself,
a tropical vine weighed
down by its fruits.

Sonnet

Eating at a restaurant where the food was all described as *young* and *tender*,
you said that you had 'absolutely nothing' to say, chewing chewing-gum.

Without looking at each other, I said, 'Did I ever tell you,' (knowing
I had), and proceeded to tell the same old story, except that I couldn't remember

it properly, thinking for a second that it might have turned out differently,
which it didn't, which isn't to say I'd change a thing, trying to decide what colour

I'd call the ceiling if forced to call it a colour. On/After the day it happened,
something moved in the darkness and I stamped on it, all morning.

What would it feel like to undergo electrocution? What was/Was that
a hovercraft? Dissecting seafood, you explained how if you walk behind

someone on a deserted street you only have to quicken your step slightly
to instil fear in the person that you're following, or about the developing

technological capabilities of rendering the artificial 'real'. When you empty
water into a vessel and then shatter the vessel the water stays, just for a moment,

where it was, no longer slightly different from itself.' Was that blood in the mayonnaise? I thought. Was that window blue on purpose?

Like a thought cut into speech, or black line next to nothing, everything echoes and then the echoes meld, like walking into a place you've just left

and not realising it's the same place or knowing why you've chosen to go in. Can't you see a face? Can't you catch a brief glimpse from a passing train,

like the trains you can't see in a Hopper painting? On/Before the day it happened, we watched that episode of *The Sopranos* (1999–2007) where Tony dreams

he's running from an angry mob and ends up riding on his horse inside the house he used to live in with Carmela. You laughed the way you laugh when you're

not really paying attention, so I imagined you getting shot in an assassination meant for someone else and went upstairs to hold on to the bathroom railings.

Without looking at each other, something moved in the darkness. Without saying anything, I thought for a second that it might have turned out differently.

Hinge

I plan to test your bright façade. Undo your second
ultrasound. I plan to take your last exam. Retract your denim miniskirt.

      Show me the empty storage vaults. Reveal the long-lost office chairs.
              Show me the burnt projector room. Your box of stolen

prison dice. Can you decide which moons to view? Which knives
to stab the tourists with? Can you explain which clouds

                to draw? Which shopping malls and streets to gild?
      Velociraptors chase the car. Some Rodins freefall through the sky.

An origami crane unfurls. This potion will restore your hearts.
I want to blanket you with snow. To watch you hijack

              someone's life. I want to shower you with blame. To
     hear that you've been stopped at last. Wake up and find yourself

embalmed! Retrieve your splintered ammonite! The park
unveils a solemn frieze. A hinge jams open swinging doors.

River:

what happens mostly is a light comes on
       and then starts getting far away from you
still lit up like an open mouth that's on
       repeat and saying *not yet* softly
not yet filling quickly like a patch of ground
       that's taken too much water in
and overflown with surplus water running off
       to some unspecified location further
on but you're already leaping forward
       too towards a sound that turns out
not to be a sound at all but merely sound
       -suggesting silence on the cusp of being
heard like something running out of life
       or running paper-footed through the house

at night and getting further and further away
       until eventually you hear that underlying
rush of noise that's always there but
       difficult to find despite how open
and continuous it is and when you do it seems
       impossible to lose because it's still
distracting you from what you thought or
       maybe hoped you'd hear if you could only
listen carefully enough to pick it out
       between these changes of direction
overtaking you one sense at a time barely
       managing to take a breath except to ask
if you could see right through me still or if
       I'd stopped or moved along

Rough Terrain

after Jorie Graham

Reading about listening to *The sounds of a crowd meaning to be silent*
and *someone breaking someone's*
fingers – just now –
didn't you say I reminded
you of someone, assuming,
that is to say, that
I wasn't the person
you were thinking
of already?
The trees were casting shadows from horizon to
horizon.
I had a feeling that
we weren't in
Kansas anymore.
I blamed it on
the boogie.
How many thousand feet above the ground is this?
you asked,
several thousand feet
above the ground,
a montage or
a montage's undoing.
She quoted at length from Wallace Stevens as I
peeled and ate a
California orange.
The segments erupted
in my mouth like
a Cy Twombly painting.
We gazed in silence at the view, which drew our eye
into the distance
as it rose
and fell in stages.
Then again, by

looking at one thing
was I missing another?
For the second time in my life an automated door
failed to open
in time
for me to make it through the parting glass. Outside, the starlings
were in murmur-
ation, newly
arrived but
already on
their way out,
thrashing apart
towards a place across the country we had never been before.
Closing my eyes,
I thought about
two sets of
hands
in three
configurations,
then of breaking
someone's fingers, then a montage breaking
up/down.

California Zephyr

Waking somewhere near
or in Nevada
from a dream of nearly

this. Behind the glass:
flattening land.
Behind that: unsuspecting

lights. Telegraph wires.
Some weaker trees.
Everything changes and then

nothing does, slipping off.
A girl reads by the window, laughing
as we reach a city

rich in unlit neon signs.
I memorize and then forget
a haiku past her

shoulder, immediately
irretrievable, still seeing for miles
over thin reflections

off the sand, still waiting for
something about to happen
to happen.

Silver and green drain
from the landscape like a worn-out
panel from a ruined church.

*Do people come out here to lose things
in the heat?*, I think, trying
to imagine seeing

us from different points
along the skyline – though by
us I must mean me. A dis-

connected voice announces
stations that we're dragged towards.
Its microphone cracks,

dying but not dead,
and I fail to recollect a line
or lines from what is

possibly a non-existent
Edward Thomas poem,
vaguer and vaguer as we

near the coast, smell the
sudden smell of salt-water,
feel the air go cold.

Kopfkino

I felt lonely, like I'd missed the boat, / or I'd found the boat and it was deserted
                                                – James Tate

Like the moment between knowing you might nearly jump
and actually nearly jumping, I considered half-undressing
an imagined Joan of Arc, approaching to the stake with faceless
soldiers and a crowd of muted children like the children in the foreground
of a Lowry painting. The only thing she could get through to me was,
It's not that I'm afraid to die, I just don't want to be there when it happens,
which, in the circumstances, we all agreed was pretty funny.

It was one of those rare experiences where you move into rain that's
already falling somewhere else. I thought about the bit in *Fargo* (1996)
where Steve Buscemi gets stuffed into the wood-chipper until only
his feet are left, imagining what that must be like those first few
seconds you're alive and whether you'd bleed out on the snow or
just lose consciousness immediately, the way some people suddenly
lose consciousness when a roller-coaster hits a loop-the-loop.

Standing before Manet's *Execution of Maximillian* (c. 1867)
in the National Gallery – damaged into sections pieced together
on a canvas in the 1990s – I watched the Emperor clasp the hand
of his companion as an officer, hardly visible, signalled to
the firing squad, vanishing behind a stage-effect of rifle smoke.
I decided that it was the best painting I had seen for a long time,
despite having seen it before somewhere, and missed it.

Someone laughed the kind of unexpected laughter that occurs
when you realise how ridiculous it is that you're disposing of a body
rolled inside a Turkish carpet, or hacked-to-bits and wrapped inside
a plastic bag to keep the blood from spoiling the upholstery in your car.
I could see a kayak heading for a hurricane, which was annoying
because I was in the kayak and I couldn't swim, or think of how
to get myself to shore. *Life is full of misery, loneliness, and suffering –*

and it's all over much too soon, I said aloud, which was annoying
because, in the circumstances, it would've been a lot funnier
if there'd been someone there to hear me say it. I could imagine
swirling around, not sure what it was that would actually kill me but
certain there'd be no way out of this one. After everything refocused,
like only realising that someone has left a room when they re-enter it,
it was late afternoon and the sun was in my eyes so I hadn't seen anything.

Fulcrum

Like a vignette, the edges
blurred by mist or smoke,

or like a thing that disappears
as soon as you touch it,

or the fractures in
a shattered elbow,

or like a moment of candlelit
clarity, as in nearly any painting
by Caravaggio,

or like a city that can
hardly be said to be there
at all but which you keep
finding yourself in,

or like the grainy, black-
and-white footage of
historical events,

or like a map of 9/11
that says both *You are here*
and *You would have been here*,

or like a completely unspatial
artwork by, for instance,
James Turrell,

or like a low-resolution
.jpg image of that artwork,

or like a mountain range
engulfed by snow,

or contrails crossing
in the evening sky,

or like saving your progress
by running into floating
crystals in the jungle,

or looking at your
photos from Slovenia, etc.,

or bonus footage
on a DVD,

or like walking past
the remnants of a club's
recent 'Hawaiian Night',

or finally turning
your back on everything,
including your family,

or like taking the fact that
you see colour perfectly
for granted,

or that, in the end, it
all comes down to
a question of
technique,

or like another (quite
different) thing that disappears
as soon as you touch it,

and the half-attentive eyes of
tourists looking back at you,

or thinking *Will I ever see
the northern lights and their
enormous shifts?*,

or wondering what those
people might be praying,
if they're praying.

The Incurables

The face that's missing from the fresco
you insist used to resemble yours. In 'The Man with the Blue Guitar',
you say, the man with the blue guitar

discusses absences as well, although it's difficult
to tell when he is singing (if he ever is) and what a difference
that would make to what he's ultimately getting at.

Equally, when we are drinking coffee in the square we see
a group of conservationists instructing eager volunteers:
*Try reaching out and contacting the hand that's reaching out
to you* – and surely that's the proof that we've been rushing
in between the two, between the proposition as it's
made and as it then comes to be understood:

the first eyes have the look of someone seeing things
a long way off; the next pair look as though
it's difficult to see.

In 'The Man with the Blue Guitar', you say, the blue guitar
surprises you unless the man himself is blue as well,
as if appearing to the world at night, his skin producing
blueness as the blue guitar produces sound.

You make adjustments to your movements
to avoid brushing against the crowd, although
it's difficult to tell whether the crowd
can even tell you're there.

I-5 North

who is more naked / than the man / yelling, 'Hey, I'm home!' / to an empty house?
— Robert Hass

About an hour from Los Angeles we pass the spot
where two weeks previously I'd seen the aftermath
of a collision. Two firefighters were joking
around, spraying suppressive foam across
dark patches of earth that had until recently been
on fire. The whole thing seemed meticulously staged.

In a photograph a man is washing blood away from
fish. A heavy knife is in the sink. His hands are
sticking to the insides of his latex gloves.
The sun grinds landscapes to a halt. It strips them
bare and crumples them like fabric, which sounds
like something Robert Hass would write.

Another picture shows a broken statue.
Large sections of the stone are missing so the stone
beneath becomes the statue's surface. The figure
looks deformed, like she's been caught in an explosion.
Out to my left, the orange groves give way to
massive oil fields. The lakes resolve a contradiction.

Driving back down to the city from
Sequoia National Park, I saw we must've passed
by the collision site again. I'd hoped that this
would turn itself to something that felt more
profound, like stepping into water
the same temperature as air.

Subtitle

The poem keeps away when I can't see or there's nothing to see
                                                              – Graham Foust

We were looking at what seemed to be nothing,
which was, in fact, nothing, gradually then suddenly gone,
fascinating the way footage of a car crash is fascinating,
or the wrongful demolition of a hospital beautiful.
There must be a better word for just exactly the wrong
word for 'accident', or 'the almost complete absence
of light from a room lighted only by the static from
a television set', waiting to be found and used –
more or less visible – in the retranslation of a film
in which the English from the mouths of the protagonist's
enemy's goons can be seen, as if intruding on itself,
surfacing too quickly to the surface of the screen
with the almost complete absence of its retranslation,
an always-certain interruption of an interruption.

What if that sky's a ceiling? That ceiling a window
not quite closed or opening? What if *What if that sky's
a ceiling?*'s a ceiling, but might as well've been clouds
emerging from, or falling behind, a sky full of clouds?
I was surprised to feel guilty, if guilty; ashamed of my
shame, if shamed. On the air I recognised a word
in Czech, left untranslated at the bottom of the screen,
appearing in italics as it was, its meaning lost, assumed
or untranslatable in kind, kind of non-existent, like a sky
painted or projected on an off-white ceiling. After
the dust cleared – the buildings resurfacing as a wave,
dormant for miles, breaks towards a peopled beach –
the room, more or less visible, seemed to slowly sink,
us still looking at nothing and then nothing again.

Ode on a Han Dynasty Urn

https://cfileonline.org/wp-content/uploads/2014/03/sujet_aiweiwei_gr-650x611.jpg

1

Sure enough, beneath a pair of hands raised in surrender,
it falls. Avoiding the parallels that we could have drawn
we watched the crowds meet in an empty square,
their many faces disappearing in the distance, blurring like
the moth-bright wings of small birds making and unmaking
flight. Like something dropping to the floor and breaking
everywhere at once – the pieces scraping underfoot – or
music punctuated by the overwhelming sound of sirens, the
scene dispersed. I bought a vase, intending to buy yellow
flowers. Smoke drifted to the coast without weight, looking
strangely poisonous. Somewhere a balloon was lifting off.
Outside we stood under an installation of fossilized trees,
listening closely to the absence of the birds, gone for
the season, leaving no trace of themselves, while you
were taking photos of the landscape like you wanted
it to move. Breaking abruptly like a water main, a rainstorm
turned your pictures into something else entirely.

2

Sure enough,   hands raised in surrender,
              the parallels
                            meet in an empty square,
              disappearing in the distance,   like
the moth-bright wings of small birds
                            dropping to the floor
                    – the pieces scraping underfoot –
       punctuated by the   sound of
                                                       yellow
flowers. Smoke   without weight,
                                          was lifting off.

Outside we stood under   trees,
listening   to the absence of the birds,

        taking photos of the landscape
        move. Breaking abruptly   a rainstorm
turned   your   pictures   into   something   else

                        3

Sure enough,
                the parallels
                            meet
                            in the distance,
            bright wings
                        dropping to the floor

                by
                                            yellow
flowers   without weight,
                                            lifting off.
Outside we stood under
                the absence of the birds,

        taking photos of the landscape
            Breaking
                    into   something   else

II

How does it feel to be outside and inside at the same time,
The delicious feeling of the air contradicting and secretly abetting
The interior warmth?

John Ashbery, 'The Bungalows'

A Few Interiors

This time we're seeing from a hiding place,
pointing stuff out – the window, heater,
Boston fern – in the interior, which is a picture
in the corner of the room, a touch unfinished,
as if an upset woman might burst in holding a letter
any minute now. The walls are white,
like a museum. There's ivy growing out from
not the top shelf but the next one down
and water in a half-drunk plastic bottle on the desk.
Within the water there's another image of the room,
reflected, bending at the sides. You can't quite
see it yet because we're standing too far
from the door, not entering for fear of
causing a disturbance. In the reflection
there's a third person as well,
but when I turn around they've gone
which is a joke I've played on you before.

The house is built among some pine trees
being cut down to make timber frames.
You sometimes hear a rifle going off
some miles away, which is a deer shot through
the neck, or just some children
killing time by firing hot rounds at the air.
Tonight there's an eclipse, but it's too cloudy
out for us to know. Instead, the empty
stairwells and the armchairs start to creak.

Divining through the long grass on the island
we find bone. Perhaps, you say, the bone's a sign,
a way of answering a problem you've been spending
your life struggling through. Back in the kitchen
it looks strange among the cutlery and tiles.
We throw it out after a day or two.

A man arrives holding a lute.
The young girl sitting takes a glance in our direction
but there's no way she can know we're here.
When she turns back her face is difficult to read;
the room becomes harmonious and bright. We let
the moment pass, insofar as we have a say, and head
into the morning with our packs and loaded guns.

In the Funhouse

In *Superman: the Movie* (1978), Superman turns back time
by flying clockwise round the globe. We see a rockslide
happen in reverse as Lois Lane emerges from the sinkhole
she's been crushed to death in, meaning that she never died
at all. In the Funhouse, a mirror shows me stretched, my head
caved in, the sole survivor of some hilarious near-fatal collision.

Halfway down an artificial indoor beach (running along a back
wall painted with what looked suspiciously like the Normandy
landings: upturned bodies on the sand, bits of bodies in the sea,
the constant sound of waves and cartoon screaming and explosions
coming from a speaker hidden somewhere in the ceiling) I wondered
if my limbs had returned to normal. The floor began to move in

circles at different speeds. The walls pressed slowly in around me.
Next door, a neon light shone on a plastic Christopher Reeve.
I made my hand into a fist and thrust it out in front of me which
did nothing, which didn't surprise anyone in the room, which
was only me, which didn't surprise anyone in the room. Crawling
through a tunnel on my hands and knees, I imagined Superman

saving me in a succession of perilous displays: trapped in the back
of a mechanically compressing car on a junkyard conveyor belt;
falling head-first from the topmost floor of a collapsing holiday
resort in Spain; cocooned in ropes and laid out on a railway track
by thugs. As I emerged, I was suddenly reminded of a scene in
a film, though couldn't remember which scene, or which film.

Colonsay

From a certain   position
it is possible to see
a strange   agitation
of light as sliding   frames
and the slight adjustments
of   falling rain assumed
into the sea with almost
imperceptible   slowness,
half-destroyed   already,
its patches   intruding on
each other as a wave
undoes the thing it's only
barely just   achieved,
mid-brushstroke,   and
the massive ships at sleep
between   two storms,
or none, or possibly   a third.
The tiny shifts in pressure,
the resistance of air   collapsing
through a window, returning
to me from a   distance
with the sensation of too many
things happening   at once,
hurling themselves away again
as a sheet of cloud unhinges
from   itself, occurring
almost   unperceived.
Patterns of stained   glass
under water,   noiseless as
a reliquary on the horizon,
or where I imagined the horizon
should have been between
the rocks,   a concrete city
rising from the ocean, losing
control of what it   motivates,

finally untangled as I felt the blood
move in my head and the sky
went whitely   on without us.

Doing Moonlight

The moon's light leaks into a halo
     as the light leaks from a television
to an unlit living room,

     as the light emits the city's stadia,
the endless crowd-noise like an untuned radio,

     or gold-leaf halos ornamenting
medieval saints in manuscripts displayed in long
     glass cases,

and the moonlight's touching everything
     and also nothing in particular.

*Use a grey brush with soft edges. Blend the birds
     and sky. Give her a mask that
looks ceramic. Give her a glove dripping
     with paint.*

An octopus is drifting to the left like rain
     that's drifting left in wind
drifting towards you,

     like rain that's drifting into snow
that's falling steadily like ash from crematoria,

     or the wing-lisps of a sparrow
wavering and turning back, as aircraft tilt away
     from dangerous weather,

the evening heaving shadows across hills now
     streaked with gold
like gold-leaf halos ornamenting medieval saints
     in manuscripts.

Start painting with the Frosted Brush.
    Make those hands erased away.
Give each layer harder light. Give her mouth
    another shape.

A nervous face is taking in the room, distorted
    as a creature is distorted by the changing
pressures of deep water,

    like an elevator rising through the floors of
an immensely sky-blent building in Dubai, the insides
    streaked with gold,

adorned with polished marble statues lining corridors
    like trees along the avenues of arboreta,
drifting to the left in wind,

    as moonlight is distorted by the billboards
lighting up the streets,

    as silence is distorted by the noise
of people gasping

    and the face that's peering in is
in the glass and looking
    blood-stained.

Add a shadow to the animals.
    Turn off all the glowing layers. Use
a basic Curves adjustment tool. Select a
    different shade of white.

The panorama widens on a bright world
    seeming to display itself,
a few points glinting like oases in the desert,

both the real and the imagined, emerging
as the light leaks from a corridor or air escapes
a punctured lung, hissing as

the late-night traffic hisses out beneath you as
you watch on from an overpass,

and the moonlight's touching everything,
drifting towards you,

and the leaves have started falling
from the trees

behind your house.

Pause, Lights, Applause

I opened the empty cabinet to find it empty.
My mother revealed that she wasn't my real father in front of a live
   studio audience.
Lady Macbeth washed her hands with and then of blood.

The figures in the paintings were coming to find themselves painted.
The figures in films, filmed. The ovenproof dog was
falsely advertised, like the ovenproof oven.

We drove a thousand miles and arrived where we had left.
Let me kill *you* for once, you said.
I chose a death worth dying for.

The landscape altered with heat, cold and pressure.
Those doors could've been heavier.
Those windows, open.

Lady Macbeth washed her hands in front of a live studio audience.
Come to think of it, I came to think of that already.
The collage was still a collage upside-down.

The waterfall was smoke. I completed the mission
with ease, without the aid of a walkthrough.
I knew the position of the guards

despite my having never seen them there before.
Three of the enemy shared a single asymmetric face.
It was always already raining.

What does it feel like to be born again?
Press *a* to fire. Press *b* to start your slow descent.
Press Δ to turn the other cheek, or laugh.

I realised that that rain would never stop.
Press O to remove your outer skin. The doors opened
with ease. The landscape emptied, slowly, like a cabinet.

Swimmers

A swimmer surfaces.
The surface of the lake is white, as if it's just been bleached,
as in the bathroom of a luxury apartment on the penthouse floor of a casino,
heavy with the smell of disinfectant.
Air conditioners fill the building with high percentages of oxygen
to make the gamblers feel more alert.
There are hardly any windows so it's hard to know what time it is.

Something's flashing in the rear-view mirror.
We were out on the peninsula, ripping at the seams like a Robert
    Motherwell painting,
watching clouds bring in the weekend's rain.
I decided to give *On the Waterfront* (1954) another go,
noticing a certain glaze to things as they passed, vaguely familiar,
like stumbling unprepared into a house you haven't been inside for years,
the light still in your eyes.

I thought of flying to Japan as an excuse to write poems with Japanese
    words in them,
looking at a map and then at photographs of Tokyo on my computer screen,
almost booking my accommodation.
Already, in the garden, our magnolia was flowering.
A picture I had taken of you swimming opened and your skin
seemed to be vitrifying. Another window
showed you wearing a kimono.

What language do you tend to speak?
Which ice cream flavours do you like the best?
Have you ever driven with the headlights off at night?
The city's falling still again, or if it wasn't we were missing out.
I was crossing a square, holding my breath,
baffled by a sudden lack of 'sights' and famous landmarks.
Another window showed me bleached

to make the gamblers feel more alert.
You were wearing a kimono / ripping at the seams
like a Robert Motherwell painting.
Whose side are you even on? Is all this really real
grass? What exactly do you mean by 'karaoke'?
There is a swimmer swimming underwater in the lake.
There is another swimmer swimming underneath / the weekend's rain.

Lacuna

just as / Nobody is looking in the right / direction in Matisse's / paintings
                                           – lines removed from the poem

Consider this: the view is empty
                    and will remain so
           for weeks. Was
there a building   there
before? Was there a park
here   with its fountain
                        splitting open?

Nobody is looking in the right
      direction. A noise is fracturing
           The space
under threat   like
      a building from an aircraft.

Between the wind turbines
                impossible to count
thinking over and over *I absolutely know*
           this   place
      the edges and straight lines
set at   impossible angles,
bringing it all sharply
           into focus. Were
we breaking the sound barrier?
Were we watching a hummingbird
there   In the garden of
           basically
                an art gallery?

A voice is   failing
           somewhere, speaking
something back to me
I've heard before.

50

Next day we sat in a café
        beneath a picture of
            a European city
bearing clouds   like
an obituary
thinking over how, now and then,
        you are always looking at me
looking down, or through
    a skylight.

                the view is empty
Between the wind turbines
lifting dust from ground
I might be   misremembering
                    as orange,
        The space
            impossible to count.
Chalk breaks
        beneath a picture of
            my fingers. Was
we breaking the sound barrier?
            an art gallery?

            A noise is fracturing
something back to me
                    splitting open
thinking over and over
Consider this
        and this and this
                and this

Portrait and a Dream

The terrain or even just the weather
changes. The yellow coach we're on is kicking dust up
from the road and everyone is happy
and having a good time, especially the woman
sitting up there at the front who keeps on
telling everyone she's *never been so far from home*.
I'm waiting for an animal to bring its heat forth
to the road, forcing the driver to pull up so we can
hear the masticating sound of something eating
something else. The guy two rows in front
(transporting fruits) is laughing his head off:
the arrangement of his many fruits is crazily precise;
a child sitting near him looks enchanted and amazed.
But Oh, isn't it curious? Haven't you found
the whole thing curious? The sunlight moving through
the house; those cooling, semi-roasted meats;
the courtyards with their shutters knocking
every night against the walls? And yes, it would be
possible to sound it out in any way you like – just think
of all the marches, long-forgotten, or the dying elephant
(hot breath, tight skin, ever so slightly bloodshot eyes),
painting her daily portrait while the audience shouts
out her name, as if to cast a kind of spell – but
in the end (and I hear somebody whispering this
even as it comes to me), still hours from the depot
which, though empty, is still brightly lit, carrying
a musty smell of animal or plant decay, a single, elderly
attendant keeping watch, reading a magazine, *You've no idea
which bit's eluding you*, at which point, hitting a bump
in the road, I tune again into the guy transporting fruits,
explaining to his neighbours how to grow a field of pineapples.

Jet Ski

Emerging switch-eyed from the undergrowth
into an evening that has just arrived but where there's still
and mainly light, at least for now, withdrawing like receding rooms,
the trees losing distinction like the faces in a crowd that's running
to or from an incident you haven't yet heard news about,
or single voices drowned out in a vast simultaneity of voices,
we see a guy pass on a jet ski, and I wonder what
he's thinking, if he's happy, where he's going, or whether he's
forgiven himself, truly, for the thing for which he's most ashamed.
Each thought feels like the answer to a question that
I've not been asked: the images of solar flares; religious
martyrs' final words; the knowledge that you're not where
you're supposed to be; another world, a bit like this.

As if to say, *Well, what did you expect?*, shrugging off
each revelation like a soothsayer who knows he's right,
the jet ski rider disappeared into the mists across the bay.
I felt an urge to drop my things and go, to follow him and start
a new life in the sun, hearing his voice say, *That's what I did,*
Baby, and look what happened to me, the wake waves
of his jet ski gently lapping on the pebbled shore.

The Excavation

Then, a few years later, a man came in and slashed the canvas
with a knife. A statement was released that used the word *unbalanced*,
which seemed fair, although we hadn't had a statement from the slasher,
who was still detained. When we got home the furniture and wall-hangings
had gone. The paint behind the frames had not been faded by the light, so
left an outline of the pictures like a kind of silhouette. I felt surprisingly
disarmed, like being caught off guard without a good excuse, unable to
give answers to the simplest set of questions: *Who are you? What are you
doing here?*, suffering a period of brief but harsh amnesia. What better
metaphor than that great city, rising from the swamp, laying its foundations
on the men who died constructing it? It makes you wonder if survivors
had a clue what they'd survived, or if the long, fantastic stories told
by nurses did the trick. One inspector wrote how the drowned horses
were *impossible to count*, and that the bridges may as well have been
constructed out of them. The thing is, as a child, I didn't know how
distance worked, that it was somehow linked to passing time and that
forgetting sometimes meant that you might live through things again,
like when you feel you're seeing mountains that you've never seen
before but then you find out from a photograph you came here
not that long ago. About a year went by in the same way. For them,
there was a chance to fix up the slashed masterpiece, re-hanging
it beside a plaque explaining what had happened. For us, there
was a chance to catch up on the things we'd missed, doing our
best to make exceptions for the minute gains and losses of each
day, which tend to sweep by unannounced the way the wind disturbs
acres of dunes. During this period we visited Lake Tahoe, which I'd only
ever seen as a relief map in a restaurant – whose outer walls were made
of plastic made to look like it was made of wood – or in *The Godfather:
Part II* (1974), because it's where the Corleones have a compound
distanced from New York. Driving north around the lake's perimeter,
I read out that its depth is over sixteen hundred feet and that (because
the water stays so cold) there could be bodies from the fifties down there,
perfectly preserved. Six yachts were sailing to the state line with their
fibreglass reflecting light. I had a vision stitched together from stock
imagery of yachting scenes: mostly bikinis and champagne and people

diving in slow motion from the yacht into the lake. Eventually, the men were discharged from the hospital. It wasn't that they'd all been cured, just that there wasn't more that could be done. It would be years before the excavation was conducted and it all made sense.

Tangerine

In the picture we were looking at
were basalt platforms fading gradually from view.

It looked like what you'd paint to try to illustrate
forgetting, or the processes of working through

an unexpected tragedy. It made me think of
tangerine, which made me think of

Frank O'Hara's poem about oranges,
especially the lines that say *The painting / is going*

on, and I go, and the days / go by, which
make me think of a revolving door.

I also thought of other words, like *redden*,
floodlit, iceberg, edge, but this was weeks later,

moving through the bright aisles of a supermarket
like a thing in an aquarium and wondering what

the constellations might be called in different
languages. The store, I found, was selling

tangerines, imported here from Israel in orange
plastic nets. Outside, the air was dusting itself off.

But me? One day I am with you somewhere
and I'm sure we've been here once before

because of shapes and trees and contours
that I recognise, and we're just sitting around

and I can see the muscles moving in your arms
which make me think of photographs by

Stephen Shore and there is music playing or just
noise, and I am thinking *What is next for you?*

about myself, *What's next for you, in your life?*,
but the futures I'm imagining are brief

and out of focus and remind me of the way
a person passing out loses the world,

which makes me think about that last scene in
The Graduate (1967) where Dustin Hoffman runs

away with Katherine Ross and they're just sitting
on the back seat of that bus not speaking

to each other and *the futures they're imagining*
are brief // and out of focus and I'm eating

Frank O'Hara's poem about oranges
because of shapes and trees and contours

we were looking at, like someone turning off
the floor and saying *ok, yeah, I get it now, I get it now,*

and I go, and the days / go by *and they're just*
sitting / on the back seat fading gradually from view,

but I am with you and I'm thinking
and, for instance, you are here

but now you're going and the days go by
and I am on my own and

Useful Phrases

I used to live here. I took these pictures. I love your accent.
See what I mean? We need to talk. Is this some kind of joke?

Does that feel good? Is this thing on? I think he might be dead.
You kissed me first. Hey, that was my idea. Are you sure this

food's Korean? We've met before. I can't stand up. I promise
this will only hurt a bit. Your place or mine? I'm really scared.

Please, give me back my wife and kids. Don't worry, this always
happens. Are you talking to me? What do you mean *pregnant*?

I wasn't born yesterday. I'm going to kill you. Are you going
to eat that? I don't want to talk about it. I hate to say this, but.

I never asked for this to happen. Do you think he's going to
show? I've got a bad feeling about this. Are you seeing what

I'm seeing? In your dreams/face. I'll have what she's having.
I love you. I'm falling. I'm going to blow up your school.

Eavesdrop

but if it doesn't have to end
    that's even better. And besides, any tidings,
        even if they did reach us, would arrive far too late, would have
become obsolete, like artefacts dug up from the ground,

the digger holding each one
    to the light and sighing, *Here is what I've found,*
        at last. But when you grow up in a small town, what's normal
to you is whatever happens within fifty miles

of your house. You can kind of
    sense it in the air, hazy like a half-recovered thought,
        but, you know, the truth of it is, if you stop and think about it,
the vastness of the space is terrifying,

2

its moorings come eventually
    adrift. One hears a great many things, true,
        but can gather nothing definite: Well, I saw a woman in a back
-yard, squawking like a chicken,

crawling on her hands and knees
    in tall, dry grass, and I saw many strange things like this.
        I feel the weight of trying to pronounce each shape, especially
a kind of square, just thinking

How do you interpret that?, coming to find
    a faded message which is meant for you and it's important, or
        it was. There is a parable which describes this situation very well:
The Emperor, so it runs,

And if it has to end, that's okay,
    too. We live enraptured by the words he said,
        the huge crowd on the lake shore, listening for days before
it somehow lost its urgency,

a sudden lapse in concentration,
    getting it down all the same. But it didn't happen like that,
        running through the coffered rooms of an Imperial palace.
The archaeologist considers

what he's found, spread out
    as if in peaceful sacrifice. On one side of a broken jar
        he sees, or hopes he sees, the maker's fingerprints,
and cries:

Leeway

The beach extends.
On second thoughts: the sky is long drawn
like a bath, or a collective intake of
breath.

A voice is saying, somewhere, *brace yourself.*
The rain completes a routine vanishing,
considering the next task
and the next.

Walking through the city
I can hear the sound of several passenger
jets, their just-descending
landing gear.

I bide my time for hours in empty, sunless
tennis courts. I feel spontaneous and
full of joy. Our sofa collapsed
like an igloo/ribcage.

Of course, a bath can only hold so much
water, you said, *like a cruise ship*
or a pair of cupping hands,
driving into

driving rain along an empty road that felt
a lot like the empty road
in a music video,
as if there must have

been people here just now
who suddenly had to go away somewhere,
hand in anxious, knowing hand.
On second thoughts:

what were we even doing here
in the first place? The sea birds came to nothing
in the end, except to
break the space like dancers

dancing on a barren hillside.
But, look: I am completely
slipping away
and that flicker might as well've been anything

being dragged from its hiding place across
the floor, and I really never
realised what was going
to happen next.

Notes

'Rough Terrain' borrows phrases from Jorie Graham's poems 'End' and 'On the Virtue of the Dead Tree'.

'Tangerine' makes use of lines from Frank O'Hara's poem 'Why I Am Not a Painter'.

'Eavesdrop' includes phrases lifted from Franz Kafka's story 'The Great Wall of China' and from several late-night talk show interviews with David Lynch conducted in the early 1990s.

Acknowledgements

I am grateful to the editors of *Blackbox Manifold, eyot, PAIN, Poetry London, PN Review* and *New Poetries VII* (Carcanet, 2018), where some of these poems first appeared.

There are a great many people – both family and friends – to whom I owe much more than I could hope to express here. Their encouragement, patience and support have been of more value to me than they could possibly know. I am very lucky.

As for the poems, it has been my immense good fortune to be instructed and inspired by some wisely critical and abundantly talented people, without whom I am certain that this book would not exist. My thanks are due especially to Adam Heardman, Isaac Nowell, Samuel Reilly, Rob Yates, Luke Allan, Vala Thorodds, Charlotte Crowe, Chloe Currens, Stephen Ross and Rebecca Chesshyre. They have all improved these poems, for which I am hugely indebted.

I would also like to thank Michael Schmidt for his vote of confidence in my work, and Aaron Aujla for lending me such a beautiful painting.